MW00512372

# TAROT FOR BEGINNERS

The 143 Pages In-Depth Yet Comprehensive Guide to Master Tarot divination, history, usage and modern decks for a Newbie or an Intermediate Level Tarot User; Become a Tarot Expert in Less Than 72 hours
Part-1

## by Kira Glent

## How to Work with this Book

For anyone willing to increase their knowledge of Tarot cards, this step by step guide to Tarots is their best bet. It is written in a manner that even with zero background knowledge of the mysticism or Tarots, with diligence, you can rival the average cartomancer.

The book opens with an introduction to the history of Tarots, enabling you to get a grip on how the cartomancy started, tracing its roots back to the early 1300s in Europe even though some scholars claim it has an even earlier origin with the Arabs.

The book goes on to explain how to gradually become an adept Tarot reader. Judiciously following the instructions in this book will have you reading Tarot cards perfectly well in no time.

Good luck!

*Tarot for Beginners*

# Table of Contents

By reading this document, the reader agrees that under no circumstances is the author responsible for any losses, direct or indirect, which are incurred as a result of the use of information contained within this document, including, but not limited to, — errors, omissions, or inaccuracies.

# INTRODUCTION

A Brief Guide to Tarot History

The tarot, known by different names through the ages, is recorded in history as early as the mid-15th century in different places in Europe. In fact, according to Tom Tadfor Little, an expert in the field, the traditional playing cards can be traced as far back as the late 1300s in Europe. It was brought from Arab countries where they have been used for much longer.

However, he mentioned that these were not Tarot cards and there are no evidence in all of history to prove that they were in existence as of this time. This simple piece of information goes against every previous narrative that seemed to say that the traditional playing cards somehow evolved from Tarot cards.

It wasn't till around the mid-1400s that the cards that most likely evolved into the Tarot cards came into existence in history. One such early mention of it in history was a letter said to be from the Duke of Milan, requesting several triumph cards to be delivered for a special event. This letter clearly differentiated the triumph cards the Duke was talking about from the regular playing cards. However, it would appear that Tarot cards were created back then as playing cards also.

Just like the traditional playing cards, tarots have four suits which are different, depending on the region. The French suits were used in Northern parts of Europe, Latin in Southern Europe, while the German suits were used in Central Europe. And just like the traditional playing cards, each tarot suit has 14 cards; 10 pip cards which are numbered from Ace (one) to ten, along with four face cards which include the King, Queen, Knight, and Knave (Jack). However, along with these, the Tarot also has a 21 -card trump suit with symbolic pictures, including one labeled as the Fool, which is not found in the traditional playing cards.

By the 14th century, the game known as "tarochhi appropriate" had become very popular among the Italian aristocracy. This game required each player being dealt random cards with which he then uses thematic associations to come up with poems about opponents. These cards were called "sortes" which means destinies.

Looking back, it can be understood that not even the earliest tarot cards were created for mysticism. They were initially created for a game that was much similar to the present-day Bridge. Back then, rich families will pay huge sums to have an artist make decks that were called "carte da trionfi" for them. These cards were known in English as "cards of triumph" and the suits were marked as cups, swords, coins, polo sticks which later became wands/staves, and a court with a king and two manservants. It wasn't until later that tarot cards came to add queens, the fool, and trumps that are unique to tarots, making the number of cards in the system add up to 78.

Nowadays, the cards have been renamed, with the suits being commonly called the Minor Arcana, while the trump cards called the Major Arcana.

## Tarot in Divination

According to graphic designer Bill Wolf who has always shown an interest in tarot designs as far back as during his high school days, there are other theories about tarot cards that aren't rooted in mysticism. According to him, the various images drawn on the cards originally had meanings that were parallel to the way the game was played, with every decision made by the players having a direct effect on how the game plays out. This is similar to the interactive novels of old where you get to choose how you want the story to go.

He explained further on how the images were created to project the important parts of the societies where the players lived in, with the prominent touch of Christianity that's visible in the symbols on the cards, showing how important Christianity was in those societies.

However, as the cards became more and more dipped in divination, the images evolved to project the intentions of its designer. They began to take on deeper meanings that were understood by fewer and fewer people while still retaining the traditional structure of four suits of pip cards that are not unlike the numbered cards in a traditional playing card, court cards, and the unique trump cards including the Fool.

All these divinatory usages of tarots, however, didn't become popular until around the late 16th century and early 17th century, albeit with a much simpler usage than how it is being used in the present day. By the 18th century, tarot cards had evolved to the extent where people had now given each card-specific meaning, with ideas on how they could be organized for divinatory purposes.

Antoine Court de Gebelin, a French Freemason and former minister, in 1781 did an analysis of the tarot and concluded that the images drawn in the tarots were actually gotten from some scarcely-known secrets of the Egyptian priests. He proceeded to say that this secret knowledge somehow arrived in Rome, where it was revealed to The Church. The Church desperately tried to keep the existence of this arcane knowledge away from the public but this obviously failed. de Gebelin later released an essay on his work where he further revealed in detail, what the tarot images translated to, connecting them to Egyptian gods like Isis, Osiris, and the rest.

However, there was a problem with de Gebelin's work. It couldn't be supported by history as there was no documentation of any of his theories. This didn't stop the wealthy from adopting the secret knowledge theory and around 19th century, it had become so widespread that card decks were being produced based on de Gebelin's theory.

Around the late 18th century, after releasing a response to de Gebelin's work and explaining how people could exploit Tarot cards for divinatory purposes, a French occultist, Jean- Baptiste Alliette, made a tarot deck that was designed specifically for divination and not just for games and entertainment.

As time went on, tarot cards got known more and more for its occultic use. This got it linked to several societies including the Kabbalah and others. Before the Victorian era reached its end, mysticism and the occult have become so popular among the upper-class families that you cannot attend a function without spotting someone reading a palm or tea leaves around somewhere.

## The Rider-Waite Deck

Arthur Edward Waite who was a British occultist and also belonged to the Order of the Golden Dawn is the creator of what may very well be the world's most popular Tarot deck. He was not only a mystic but also a spiritual seeker who also consulted as a writer and translator. He published a book in 1889 with the alias, Grand Orient. The book that was titled "A Handbook of Cartomancy, Fortune-Telling and Occult Divination", was among the earliest books written in English as a guide to Tarot reading.

Arthur Waite was very fascinated with the occult and it was for this reason that he joined the Hermetic Order of the Golden Dawn. However, with time, his spirituality gradually evolved, moving him towards Christian mysticism. The moment the Golden Dawn broke, he rallied up some people and created his own order known as the Fellowship of the Rosy cross. And in 1909, he teamed up with an artist, Pamela Colman Smith who was also belonged to the Golden Dawn, to create what is now known to be the Rider-Waite deck.

Following Waite's request, Smith drew inspiration from the Sola Busca artwork which shares a lot of similarities with her final work. She was the very first artist to incorporate characters into the images of the lower cards. As opposed to merely painting the cups, wands, coins, or swords, she added images of people into it, resulting in the popular deck that we all know and recognize today.

Due to its similarity with Kabbalistic symbolism, this deck is the go-to deck for almost every instructional book on the Tarot. Nowadays, the deck is widely known as the Waite-Smith deck, in a bit to recognize Smith's contribution to the work.

With over a century gone since the release of the Rider-Waite deck, Tarots have gone through a lot of evolution and are now available in so many more designs. Although each card is adapted to its designer's theme, they all share similarities with the Rider-Waite deck.

In the present day, Tarot has evolved from being exclusive to the wealthy upper-class families of the society to being easily accessible by anyone who is willing to learn about it.

Hidden Knowledge: Kabbalah and Astrology

According to the Oxford dictionary, the Kabbalah is an ancient Jewish tradition of mystical understanding of the Bible which was originally passed down through word of mouth, by means of ciphers and other secret methods. It got really popular just when the Middle Ages was ending and is still quite significant in Hasidism.

It is believed to be a pearl of ancient wisdom that teaches believers the secrets that make the universe tick. The word Kabbalah literally means "to receive".

However, it's necessary to know that Kabbalah's teachings are not about finding yourself. It is more like losing oneself, so as to become one with the universe.

Don't be confused. Look at it this way. Kabbalah is about receiving an understanding that exceeds what an average human is capable of achieving. However, before one can be receptive to the higher consciousness, he or she needs to first become receptive, losing himself in the universe so as to become one with it.

It is quite necessary to note that some scholars believe the Kabbalah to be of three different types which include;

- The Magical: is rooted in the ability to alter and influence how nature occurs. It makes use of incantations, amulets, Divine names, amongst other things to make this possible.

- The Meditative: is concerned with helping users achieve higher consciousness by means of meditation. With this, you can even reach a prophetic state.

- The Theoretical: this category is majorly concerned with the inner dimensions of reality, that is, the spiritual worlds, angels, souls, and so on.

Thinking about these different categories of the kabbalah, it will be noted that the magical kabbalah has very few texts in existence. This might be due to its complexity, the fact that it is quite difficult to master, and even the dangers it posed to those who had mastered it. It's said that R. Joseph Della Reina (1418 – 1472), who was a great master of the magical kabbalah, once attempted to use his spiritual ability to achieve ultimate redemption but failed woefully in the process. This failure led to him becoming spiritually injured, thus, keeping others at bay from following in his footsteps. From that moment onward, the magical kabbalah had gradually spiraled into extinction.

One would also quickly notice from research that the meditative kabbalah had never been popular among believers. Those who practice it make use of meditation to achieve higher consciousness. One notable advocate of this category of kabbalah, R, Abraham Abulafia (1240 – 1296), was of the school that his method of writing a mantra to meditate was very efficient in attaining a level of prophecy. His method consisted of repeatedly writing a word in various forms, altering the way the words are written by permuting and cycling the letters, composing new motifs of letters, and so on, till a higher consciousness is achieved.

However, Abulafia's never published any of his works as most of the great kabbalists of his time were against him and his teachings. Therefore, his method of practicing Meditative Kabbalah was never able to become mainstream even though individual kabbalists have been known to make use of his teaching to achieve transcendence.

The most popular Kabbalah is the theoretical type and it consists of most of the Kabbalah. It follows the sacred teachings of the book Zohar which was written by the 2nd-century Talmudic mystic, Rabbi Shimon Bar Yochai. This book was initially handed down through the generation till the 13th century when it got published by kabbalist, R. Moshe De Leon.

Among the many parts of this Kabbalah is the kabbalistic astrology.

Astrology, however, is an ancient means of learning how the planetary movement affects our lives, from work to love life and everything in between. Understanding how the universe affects our lives gives us an edge over how to make decisions that affect our lives.

There are different types of astrology practiced in the world today. There is the Esoteric Astrology, Jyotish or Vedic astrology, Shamanic astrology, and so on. And one of such many different types of astrology is the kabbalistic astrology.

In all types of astrology, the knowledge you receive from an astrological reading will help in showing you how best to achieve your potentials. You do not only get to learn and understand yourself better, but you also get to know how to best communicate and express yourself while also learning how to best interact with other people. Everyone has their own special abilities and challenges that are peculiar to their astrological signs. The signs are more or fewer guides, sensitizing us about our challenges and goals. However, Kabbalistic astrology goes further on to teach us how to rise above the cosmic powers and be the pilots of our own lives.

Astrology is also quite important in tarot reading. Knowing which cards represent which signs will help you give an accurate reading, and thus a more accurate description of people. Every sign in the zodiac is represented by a corresponding card in the major arcana. Also, each suit of the minor arcana represents an element and as such, the elements are represented by the zodiac signs.

- Cups represent the water element and the corresponding zodiac signs are Cancer, Scorpio, and Pisces.
- Wands represent the fire element and the corresponding zodiac signs are Leo, Aries, and Sagittarius.
- Swords are connected with Air and the air signs are Gemini, Libra, and Aquarius.
- Pentacles represent Earth and the earth signs include Taurus, Virgo, and Capricorn.

The minor arcana also have connections to the signs. They are very helpful when you need to establish which zodiac sign a court card represents instead of the element. However, every court card can be connected to the age or maturity level of the person being read.

- Pages: kids or people who are young at heart

- Knights: young adults or people who are want to start all over

- Queens: women who have reached maturity or with emotional maturity.

- Kings: men who are matured or people who are grounded and have the attributes of a good leader.

Also, the court cards each have an element they represent. This means that even though the person whom the card represents might have a certain zodiac sign, they could still be influenced by the element represented by that card.

- Pages element is Earth

- Kings represent Fire

- Queens represent Water

- Knights represent Air

# PART 1
# The Modern Tarot Deck

Arcana, as it were, is derived from the Latin word *Arcanum* which is said to mean secret or closed. Another origin of the word is from the French word *area*. The word area also means chest as well as container, box or in some cases ark. Another very interesting definition of the word arcana and indeed Arcanum is "mystery of mysteries". Now, this was also said to mean a revelation of the greatest secret in occultic art, sciences, and interestingly enough, tarot, astrology, alchemy and many other specialties. The word arcana also simply means highly specialized and classified. Something that is known only to a highly regarded and select few. In the occult world, the word means very mysterious knowledge or information that is shared only to the initiated ones. Some circles also use it to mean powerful medicine or elixir. By association, the Major Arcana simply means the biggest of secrets and mysteries. Arcana in tarot terms, however, means a grouping of cards.

## The Major Arcana

There are seventy-eight cards in a typical Tarot deck. The seventy-eight cards are then split into two very distinct groups that each have different functions. The first group is the Major Arcana and the second is called the Minor Arcana. The Major Arcana cards deal more with significant events, massive changes, and major event shifts. Whereas, the Minor Arcana cards deal more with daily experiences and minor shifts and changes in a person's life.

The Major Arcana are the cards that carry mostly symbolic characteristics in a deck of typical tarot cards. They are made up of 22 cards out of the 78 cards in a deck. These symbolic cards are also known as trump cards or Arcanum when they are placed individually and are usually numbered from 0 to 21. The Major Arcana or trumps were mostly used in gaming situations before the 17th century. The wealthier strata of society used them for friendly games and gambling. The trumps never really had any cultural or allegorical connotations when they were first used. However, when a Tarot deck is used in a game, the Major Arcana serve as the permanent trumps, which means that they are elevated above the other cards. They carry more complex connotations and seem to carry big themes and expansive archetypal influences. Influences that could guide and/or ultimately change the course of a life and soul's journey towards broader senses and enlightenment.

One Major Arcana origin story says that the trumps came from triumphs, the ancient card game called Trionfi, which was mostly adopted in France and Italy at the time. In typical game situations, the trump cards would outrank every other card in the game. A school of thought says that the cards not only carry deep meanings and instructions for life passed down from ancient times, but also carry key elements of human consciousness that are to be followed and paid attention to.

Another origin story says that they are derived from a Milanese carnival based on the Roman festival of Saturnalia. Then, urban dwellers would dress up in fine clothes and parade throughout the city with convoys of chariots during the festivities. Some people believe that the then Duke of Milan commissioned some of the earliest cards in the fifteenth century namely "the Visconti -Sforza tarot cards". Charles VI of France is goes down in history as the owner of the very first tarot deck which is in line with perceptions about him being a lover of mystic things, passionate distractions, and pageantry.

A group of tarot cards contains vital and important information about a person that when revealed, serves the purpose of answering the big questions like a person's fate, secret mysteries of the universe, and where a person's place is in the big picture.

The Fool is a constant image among the Trump cards. It is the only unnumbered card among them. The Major Arcana follows the fool's journey. It follows as he goes along to meet new adventures and characters, he learns new lessons and takes different turns as he makes his journey through all the cards. This journey eventually concludes when he gets to the World Card.

One of the characteristics of the Major Arcana to always remember is that it lays out a more or less spiritual path. The major arcana illustrates, in picture form, the path that anyone on any spiritual path follows or evolves through to higher consciousness. This is one reason the tarot can be a powerful adjunct to whatever spiritual path you may already be following.

The major arcana also depicts a storyline that follows the fool's journey which plays out human development. It can actually be described as multiple lifetimes. There some people who look at the major arcana in terms of archetypes. They see them in ways of thinking, ways of feeling, and in ways that human beings react in response to internal and external stimuli. Spiritual psychologists are known for making this association.

Another way to describe the major arcana is that it pictorially displays the natural laws and principles of the universe. It also shows a depiction of the results that follow when a life is lived according to these principles.

The major arcana can also be seen as a chest of mystical and spiritual wisdom. Mystics also associate the 22 cards with the Hebrew alphabet, with each card being a pictorial explanation of each alphabet. The cards of the major arcana can be described as representing the basic principles of an evolved universe. This is described as the "cube of space". In Hebrew, it is called Sepher Yetzirah, or "Book of Creation," and has been used by Kabbalists for a very long time. The cube has typical geometrical cube attributes, with 22 dimensions, 12 sides, 6 faces, 3 axes, and 1 center. These 22 dimensions along with the Hebrew alphabets and the cards that constitute the major arcana correspond with one another. The Kabbalists believe the major arcana holds the standard key that unlocks the door to higher consciousness and an awareness oh unseen things.

## The Minor Arcana

The remaining cards in a tarot deck are referred to as the minor arcana. Similar to traditional playing cards, they can be split up into four suits, which are also called tools. These suits include wands, cups, swords, and pentacles. In each Suit, there are fourteen cards numbered from Ace to Ten, along with four court cards, bringing their total to fourteen cards. The court cards are the Page, Knight, Queen, and King. The four suits each have a specific ruling element and each of them corresponds to very specific and distinct areas of life. The names of these Suits all originated from the Middle Ages and are said to represent different classes of people. The wands represent agricultural depictions namely: staffs or cudgels which are seen as weapons synonymous with peasant lifestyle. The cups take on a holy representation, signifying sacred vessels and in turn the clergy at the time. The swords as you would have guessed, signify war or soldiers going to war. And the pentacles or means of commerce (money) signify the businessmen or merchants. The four suits represent the four elements with the wands representing fire, the cups representing water, the swords representing air and the pentacles representing earth.

# PART 2

# Introduction to the Cards

The cards are an extremely major part of Tarot reading as they are the medium through which the readings are made. A traditional Tarot card deck has 78 cards: 22 in the Major Arcana and 56 in the Minor Arcana.

The cards in the Major Arcana are symbolic images that are the most significant for the reading while those in the Minor Arcana are used to give more context to the symbolism of the Major Arcana cards during reading. Simply put, the Major Arcana cards give the large but important unspecified readings while the Minor

Arcana cards refine the readings of the Major Arcana.

The cards all have picture scene that has a symbolic meaning. While the depiction of the image might vary from different decks, they share a similarity that ensures that the symbolic meaning remains the same across all decks. The Major Arcana cards typically have an image that may have a name and number or not while the Minor Arcana cards which are similar to the cards on a traditional deck also have images and are also divided into four different suits with each suit consisting of 14 cards. The image in the card gives a direct representation of the suit and number the card is representing.

The four suits of the cards in the Minor Arcana all have a specific element, class, and faculty attached to it. The four suits can either be the common French Suit or the Latin Suit. For the purpose of this section, the Latin Suit will be used but the corresponding French Suit will be stated along with the element, class, and faculty of each suit.

### WANDS (Clubs)

The Wands Suit corresponds to Clubs in French Suit. It holds fourteen cards which include the numbers one to ten then a *Page* , *Knight, Queen,* and *King.* The Page and Knight are sometimes called *Princess* and *Prince*. The number one is called *Ace*. The *Suit of Wands* can also be called *Suit of Batons* or *Suit of Staves*.

The Suit of Wands has the element attribute of *Fire*, a class attribute of *Artisans* and a faculty attribute of *Creativity and Will.*

### COINS (Diamonds)

The Coins Suit corresponds to Diamonds in French Suit. It holds fourteen cards which include the numbers one to ten then a *Page, Knight, Queen,* and *King*. The Page and Knight are sometimes called *Princess* and *Prince*. The number one is called *Ace*. The *Suit of Coins* can also be called *Suit of Disks, Suit of Rings* or *Suit of Pentacles*.

The Suit of Coins has the element attribute of *Earth*, a class attribute of *Merchants* and a faculty attribute of *Material Possessions.*

### CUPS (Hearts)

The Cups Suit corresponds to Hearts in French Suit. It holds fourteen cards which include the numbers one to ten then a *Page, Knight, Queen,* and *King*. The Page and Knight are sometimes called *Princess* and *Prince*. The number one is called *Ace*. The *Suit of Cups* can also be called *Suit of Chalices*.

The Suit of Cups has the element attribute of *Water*, a class attribute of *Clergy* and a faculty attribute of *Emotions and Love*.

## SWORDS (Spades)

The Swords Suit corresponds to Spades in French Suit. It holds fourteen cards which include the numbers one to ten then a *Page*, *Knight*, *Queen,* and *King*. The Page and Knight are sometimes called *Princess* and *Prince*. The number one is called *Ace*.

The Suit of Swords has the element attribute of *Air*, a class attribute of *Nobility and Military*
and a faculty attribute of *Reason*.

The Suit of Swords deals with mental consciousness centered on the mind and intellect. The swords are often sharpened on both sides, symbolizing the balance of dominion and brains and how they can be applied either towards good deeds or evil ones. A balance with Spirit (Wands) and Feelings (Cups) is needed for a very positive effect.

The element of this suit is Air and just as air is in constant movement, the suits also represent change along with power, action, and knowledge. The suits resonate strongly with those born under the astrological sign of Air; Aquarius, Libra, and

Gemini. They can be intelligent, rational and logical and on the flip side, ruthless, domineering and rigid.

## The Cards of the Major Arcana

As earlier stated, the major arcana is composed of 22 cards. Going

by the Rider-Waite-Smith deck, the cards are arranged thus:

# The Fool

Upright: New beginnings, Innocence, Free Spirit, Spontaneity
Reversed: Risk-taking, Holding back, Recklessness

This card can start or end of the deck as its number is 0 and therefore doesn't have a permanent place from either of the two options. It's a card with unlimited potential as it signifies a clean slate. As the whole deck is sometimes interpreted as "a fool's journey through life", this card signifies new beginnings of a journey.

The card features a beau staring out from the edge of a cliff. He seems to be without a care and looks set to embark on an adventure. In his right hand is a small bag tied to a stick and it is slung over his shoulder and it contains all he needs. He is gazing at the universe (skywards) and looks unaware that he is about to fall off the cliff's edge into the unknown. His left hand holds a white rose which represents his innocence and purity and a small dog at his feet which signifies loyalty and protection. The mountain in the background signifies future

challenges but the Fool's attitude shows he's not concerned with them right that moment and is rather focused on the new adventure that awaits.

Upright: When the card is upright, it signifies new beginnings, opportunities, and potential. It is a sign that you are starting a journey into the unknown and trusting the universe to take you on an adventure that you are committed to even though it might seem crazy. The Fool encourages you to be curious, open-minded and adventurous on this new journey. Forgo the anxiety and worries of what may be or not and sink yourself into the experience and excitement coming your way. The card is a sign to take action on a new endeavor even if you feel you don't have all you need. Be creative with what you have and let spontaneity guide you on this adventure. Go with the flow, have fun and relax. Embrace your carefree spirit and unlimited potential and don't let the doubt of details hold you back. Take a chance and trust the universe to catch you as you fall off the precipice into this new adventure.

Reversed: The reversed Fool card can signify that you are moving too fast too soon. In an attempt to be free and trust the universe, you are committing to too many risks and thoughtless actions without considering the consequences on yourself and others. The card calls you to slow down and take stock of yourself and your adventure. As you trust the universe, let your actions also show that the universe can trust you. The reversed Fool can also signify indecision and hesitation. You are letting too many thoughts cloud your free-spirited nature and are holding back from embarking on your adventure. While forethought and caution are okay, don't use it as an excuse to hold onto the past rather than explore the unknown of the future. The reversed Fool urges you not to be "a Fool"

## The Magician

Upright: Inspired action, Manifestation, Power, Resourcefulness

Reversed: Untapped talents, Poor planning, Manipulation

The Magician is numbered 1 in the deck and that is a number that represents new beginnings and opportunities. The Magician has his right hand stretched upwards (skywards) to the universe and his left hand pointing to the earth. This signifies his connection to both the cosmic and physical realm. He uses this connection to tap into energy from the cosmic realm to create matter in the earthly realm. His white robe signifies purity while his red cloak signifies knowledge and experience of the world.

On the table are objects symbolizing each suit of the Tarot with each representing an element (Wands for Fire, Coins for Earth, Cup for Water and Sword for Air). This signifies that he has the resources needed to manifest his thoughts into action. Above him is an infinity symbol and around his waist is a snake swallowing its tails and this both signify unlimited potential. The foreground contains an array of blossoming flowers that symbolize the fruition and blossoming of his ideas.

Upright: As a master of making his thoughts a reality along with having all the tools, energy and potential, The Magician signifies that you have all the resources to realize your dreams into reality. You have spiritual energy (Fire), physical energy (earth), mental energy (air) and emotional energy (water). It signifies that it is a perfect time to go ahead a make a dream into a reality. You have everything you need to make your dreams become a reality and you are ready. Tap into the unlimited potential and energy at your disposal, establish a clear image of your goals and take the necessary steps towards achieving it. Remember, it is not only about having the energy, resources, and potential. You also have to take action and seize control.

Focus and commit to the task at hand and take steps to manifest your dreams into reality. You are the master of your fate.

Reversed: On one hand, the reverse Magician can signify that you are exploring an idea to make into reality but are yet to take action to pursue it. You are being limited by your doubts in your own ability to make it work with the resources at your disposal. Trust yourself and stay awake to the signs around you for the opportunities they can bring. On another hand, the reverse magician can signify a struggle to accomplish a current goal. You either don't know where to begin or what the next step to take is. You have failed to create a clear mental image of what your goals are and you are suffering from poor planning. Or you have lost touch with why the goal is important and no longer feel joy in following that path, therefore the universe is telling you to look back before you continue forward. At its worst, the reversed Magician signifies greed and manipulation. You are achieving your dreams to the detriment of others and doing it solely for your personal gain. This can either be intentional or unintentional. It can also mean untapped potential in hat you have all the resources and are the one holding yourself back from achieving your dreams.

The High Priestess

Upright: Divine Feminine, Sacred Knowledge, Intuition, Subconscious mind Reversed: Secrets, Disconnection from Intuition, Silence, Withdrawal

The High Priestess sits with a veil designed with pomegranates behind her. The veil represents the barrier between the conscious

45

and the subconscious, and it is, therefore, a barrier against those who aren't willing to look deeply enough. The pomegranates on the veil symbolize abundance, fertility and the divine feminine. On both sides of her stands two pillars that signify the entrance to the temple shrouded in mystery (associated with the Temple of Solomon). The pillar to her right is black and has the letter "B" inscribed on it.

The pillar to her left is white and the letter "J" inscribed on it. The letter "B" stands for "Boaz" which means "in his strength" while the letter "J" stands for "Jachin" which means "he will establish". The Black and White symbolize duality; darkness and light, masculine and feminine, right and wrong. The entire ensemble signifies that knowledge and acceptance of duality (open-mindedness) are required to enter the hallowed grounds of the temple.

She wears blue robes with a white cross on her chest and a horned crown. These all signify her leadership in matters of the Divine with divine knowledge. She has a scroll in her hands with the letters TORA and her hand rests on her lap. The scroll which signifies greater law is partially concealed to show that sacred knowledge is only shown to those willing to look outside the earthly realm. The crescent moon at her feet symbolizes her intuition and subconscious mind and the natural cycles of the moon.

Upright: she is a teacher of sacred knowledge and hidden mysticism and the guardian of the subconscious. She sits on the pathway between the conscious and subconscious realms and can travel to both effortlessly. She offers a deep understanding of the universe through increased awareness of secret knowledge which she guides willing open-minded students into through a thin veil of awareness. She signifies spiritual enlightenment, divine knowledge, and wisdom. Her appearance reminds you to seek knowledge deep within and tune into your intuition because the answer you are seeking is a truth you have known all along. She guides you as you become aware of your consciousness and wisdom and venture into your subconscious mind. Synchronize with your inner wisdom and Higher Self through visualization, meditation, and spiritual journeys.

Trust in your intuition and allow it flow. Embrace your divine feminine; wisdom, empathy, compassion. No matter your gender, embracing your divine feminine will ensure you find the balance between your masculine and feminine energies. Embrace your ability to trust, nurture and empathize.

Reversed: The reversed High Priestess advises you to stop and reflect inwards, to listen to your intuition and wisdom. Withdraw yourself from the noise around you and listen to your inner voice. Don't doubt what your intuition is telling you even if people's opinions ad reason might run contrary. Trust in what the universe is telling you through your intuition.

Her secretive nature may suggest gossip or hidden agenda. Trust in your wisdom to expose and resolve these secrets and do not give in to paranoia or assumptions. It can also mean knowing when to share information and when to keep it a secret.

The Empress

Upright: Nature, Abundance, Feminity, Nurturing, Beauty

Reversed: Dependence on others, Creative block.

The Empress a beautiful, curvy woman with blond hair and a gentle demeanor. On her head is a crown of twelve stars which signifies her connection to the mystical realm and the cycles of the natural world. The twelve stars, however, signifies the months of the year and planets. She dons a white robe patterned with pomegranates which symbolize innocence and fertility and she sits on a luxurious arrangement of flowing red velvet and cushions. One cushion has a symbol of Venus which symbolizes love and it is symbolic of fertility, beauty, grace – all these which are attributes of The Empress.

A vibrant forest ad winding stream surround her to signify her connection to the Earth, nature, and life. Golden wheat in the foreground reflects abundance for harvest.

Upright: It is a sign of a powerful connection to feminity which translates to elegance, sensuality, fertility, nurturing, etc. all of which are necessary to create a balance between man and woman. You are urged to synchronize with your feminity. Connect with beauty. Tap into your senses and experience pleasure and fulfillment from your environment. Express yourself and be creative through art forms. Apply yourself to a new hobby that will tap into and improve your creativity.

The Empress also signifies abundance. Reflect on the beauty of abundance around you and take pleasures in the luxuries that life is offering. As an archetype of Mother Earth, The Empress also encourages you to involve yourself in nature and sync with its energy. When this happens, you'll take in Mother Nature's caring nature and feel love, compassion and the urge to care for others.

This can also suggest pregnancy, birth or stepping into a mothering role. Birth and pregnancy can be literal or metaphorical in the sense of coming up with a new goal or even a sense of self.

Reversed: The reversed Empress encourages you to prioritize yourself. Love and care for yourself and focus on caring for your needs. It can also suggest a creative block in birthing a new idea or in creative expression. Don't bother with what people think and express yourself in ways that make you happy. The card may also make you aware of your body image. It asks you to love yourself and recognize your beauty inside and out. Don't depend on other people's perception of how you see the beauty in yourself and others.

The Emperor

Upright: Power, Organization, Form, Father figure, Masculinity

Reversed: Sovereignty, Excessive dominance, Lack of discipline, Inflexibility

In contrast to the mother archetype of The Empress, The Emperor is a father. He sits on a stone throne designed with four ram heads which symbolizes his connection to Aries and the planet Mars. He holds an "ankh" in his right hand and an orb in his left. The ankh symbolizes life while the orb symbolizes the world he rules over. He wears armor to portray his strength and to show that he is protected from harm and over the armor is a red robe that symbolizes his energy, passion, and power. His white beard symbolizes his wisdom acquired from age and experience and his gold crown symbolizes his authority.

A looming mountain range with a flowing river at its base is in the background. The mountain symbolizes and solid foundation that can be immovable but the river gives a contrast that there exists a gentler side if one were to search for it in the midst of all the rigidity. The card suggests you are adopting a fatherly role, regardless of your gender. You are providing for and protecting your loved ones. People attribute a sense of stability and security to you. The card also suggests your comfortability with respect and authority. You are fit to lead and you do it firmly but fairly. You listen to others but have the final say. You are always ready to protect those important to you from danger and people know they can rely on you.

Upright: The Emperor represents a system of law and order. You create order from chaos and enforce rules and regulations. You don't rush into situations without a plan but rather figure out an approach that is effective and efficient. Emperor signifies wisdom through experiences. You have passed through trials and come out the other side stronger and wiser and can, therefore, offer guidance and direction to those around you.

Reversed: The reversed Emperor asks you to re-evaluate your relationship with power and authority. It can also symbolize a misuse of power or authoritarian behaviors from you or those around you. It may also be a sign of inflexibility and an unwillingness to listen to the advice of others. Also, it represents a lack of authority causing a gradual collapse in the system. You may have lost a sense of direction because you have lost an authority figure or you have given away your power or compromised your authority to either please others or for selfish gain. It can also be a sign of unwillingness to take on the leadership role or father figure despite being in a position to do so.

The Hierophan

Upright: Spiritual wisdom, Tradition, Religious beliefs, Conformity, Rules Reversed: Personal belief, Challenging the status quo, Freedom.

He is alternatively called The Pope or The Teacher in some decks and is ruled by Taurus. This is the masculine counterpart of The High Priestess. Although different from that of the High Priestess, the religious figure sits between the pillars of a temple. The Hierophant wears three robes of colors red, blue and white. He also wears a three layers crown. This double trinity in his attire represents the three realms he rules; the conscious, subconscious and superconscious. He holds a Papal cross in his left hand and raises the other in a fashion of religious blessing with two fingers pointing to the heavens and two fingers pointing down at the earth. The cross in his left hand is a triple scepter that signifies religious status. Kneeling before you are two followers who signify initiates that The Hierophant is to instill his spiritual wisdom into so they can be appointed to roles in the temple. The entire ensemble denotes a shared identity among the characters and a ceremony to rise through the ranks. The keys crossed at the Hierophant's feet represent the unlocking of mysteries only the Hierophant can access and impart on others, and also the balance between the conscious and subconscious.

Upright: The Hierophant represents a detailed and structured set of spiritual beliefs and values that are often associated with religious and similar doctrines. The Hierophant urges you to study the fundamental principles of any doctrine from a learned source before you discover your own path and make your choices. Work with a mentor to open you to the realm of spiritual doctrines with their values and beliefs so he can nurture your spiritual growth and awareness and help you access the Divine through an understanding of traditions and core principles. If you have mastered the teachings, then it is time for you to become a teacher and guide others through their own journey. Honor and accept the responsibility to pass down

structured knowledge while respecting the age-old traditions that govern it. The Hierophant suggests that you follow a beaten path and staying within its boundaries. You stick to a known idea that guarantees success and doesn't go out of your way to create something new. The Hierophant may call on you to honor the family value and sacred tradition in their original form. If you are lacking a sacred tradition, you can create one. It can be as simple as doing following a specific routine every day. Explore your spiritual self. This card is about identifying with others within a structured set of traditions and known values. Explore communities you can join, either spiritual or otherwise that will give you a sense of belonging.

Reversed: In its best form, The Hierophant urges you to remember that you are knowledgeable enough to teach yourself. You don't need an external source of wisdom. You are knowledgeable enough to make your own path or choose what to believe without external influences. It may finally be time to go against established traditions and forge a new path.

Trust in yourself and your deep knowledge. You no longer need external approval in the choices you make with the path you take.

The Hierophant card is about not conforming. It's time for you to test and challenge the ideas you have always believed to be true.

You seek your truth and break the rigid tradition that might be constraining you. You found your true spiritual self. It is time to stop following the crowd that you have always believed to be right and time to look for the path that is right for you. You might run up against authority figures of the prior values you hold but don't let it deter you from your truth.

## The Lovers

Upright: Love, Harmony, Romance, Relationship, Value alignment, Choices Reversed: Imbalance, Self-love, Misalignment of values, Disharmony

The Lovers card shows a nude man and woman standing under an angel whom the woman is gazing at. The angel is Raphael meaning "God heals" and represents spiritual and physical healing. The angels bless their union and remind them of their connection with the Divine.

The couple stand in a beautiful, bountiful landscape reminiscent of the Garden of Eden. Right behind the woman is a tall fruitful apple tree with a serpent coiling its way to the top. This represents the promise of pleasure that can take one's focus away from the Divine. Behind the man is a tree of flames which represent passion. The twelve flames on the tree suggest the twelve zodiacs, the symbols of time and eternity. The man gazes at the woman who gazes at the angel representing a path from physical desire to the emotional need to spiritual concern. The phallic-looking volcano represents the eruption of passion waiting to happen between the man and woman. The angel can also be seen as keeping the couple apart. The man has noticed the woman who is yet to notice him but the phallic volcano indicates the passionate eruption that will erupt between them when she finally lowers her gaze and notices the man. The card implies Agape love with a likely promise of Eros.

Upright: In its best form, The Lovers card represents conscious connections and meaningful relationships. The card indicates a close meaningful relationship with somebody. It could be a romantic relationship or close friendship or even family. This card is about honesty and communication. The nudity of the couple indicates that they are laid bare to their most vulnerable and are open to sharing their all with each other. This creates a bond forged by trust and confidence. This signifies that open and honest communication with those you care about will create beautiful and strong relationships forged with the fires of trust and respect.

The card also represents clear and concrete personal beliefs and values. It has a slight connection with The Hierophant and you taking a stand in your beliefs after learning and acquiring knowledge. You are choosing who you are, staying true to who you are and loving who you are. The card also indicates a choice. A choice on who you can be, how you want our relationship with people to be and what values you want to emulate and portray. You pick the values you prefer being known for and stick to them. You are going for the best version of yourself. The card also encourages you to unify opposing forces to create a whole. Unify the positives and negatives, accept the advantages and disadvantages, etc. When you do this, you can create a new beautiful unification from which love can take root and sprout.

Reversed: A reversed Lover card can signal a time you are out of sync with your loved ones. Relationships and communications are getting harder to maintain and you no longer connect with your loved ones. It is time to let go and move on or find that spark once more and rekindle your relationships. However, whatever choice you make, do what is best for you.

The reversed card can also reflect one-sided feelings in a relationship from either side of it. It also speaks of self-love and respect. Honor your own values and accept who you are.

Understand how different you are from others and recognize the traits you want to emulate in others is one that you already have yourself. It can also indicate conflicts especially with regards to your choices and values. You might have to make a tough choice that might conflict with your values. You might be at disharmony within yourself. This is where you might have to re-evaluate your values and choices. It can be a good point at which you refer back to The Hierophant and seek advice and guidance from an institution or spiritual guide.

At its worst, a reversed Lovers card is an indication of emotional distress from divorce, break-up, and split-up. It may be a suggestion for the need to re-evaluate your present romantic relationships and rekindle it.

# Chariot

Upright: Action, Willpower, Determination, Success, Control
Reversed: Opposition, Self-discipline, Lack of direction

The card shows a warrior in a chariot. He dons an armor adorned with crescent moons which represent "what is coming into being", a tunic with a square which represents "strength of will" and other symbols that represent spiritual transformation. The star and laurel crown signify success, victory and spiritual evolution. He has a magician like wan that signifies his control over the chariot comes from his will of mind as he holds no reins. His standing stance indicates his proactive nature in taking action and moving forward. The canopy above him is adorned with six-pointed stars suggesting a connection to the Divine Will and the Celestial world. Two sphinxes of black and white sit in front of his chariot representing duality. They also suggest opposing forces with their color scheme and the fact that they are going in either directions. However, the charioteer is in charge and can steer the chariot in any direction he wants through his force of will. Behind the chariot is a river representing the need to float with the stream of the universe while also being in command of the direction he is going.

Upright: This card represents willpower, strength, and determination. Just as The Lovers card has shown you how to choose your values, this card indicates that it is time to take action on those choices. The card is a sign of encouragement, a nudge that you should dedicate yourself to achieving your objectives. Apply willpower, commitment, and discipline on your path to achieve your aims and objectives successfully. Stop taking a passive path hoping things will work out. Get up, get active and proceed to achieve your goals no matter the challenges that may come your way. Even if you are being pulled in different directions and find you are faltering, believe in yourself and find that strength and willpower to make your goals a reality. If you are already working to achieve your dreams, the chariot is a sign to persevere, concentrate and remain confident. Don't search for shortcuts. Accept the test of strength, conviction, and willpower, thrown your way and follow through to victory. Be confident and courageous. Boldly express your desires and set your boundaries. Have faith and believe in your strength.

Reversed: Where the upright Chariot indicates an encouragement to move ahead, the reverse Chariot is a sign to go back. Turn a blind eye rather than doggedly moving in your current direction or re-evaluate your goals and see if a change is to be made. The reversed Chariot can be a warning that you are allowing the challenges in your path to get the better of you and prevent you from making your goals a reality. It is time to reaffirm your commitments and push through your challenges. Take greater control over your destiny. Focus on what you can control, and for what you can't, take this opportunity to improve yourself in a bid to achieve more control. However, don't fall into the trap of exerting too much control. Sometimes it is good to allow the universe to be in control and let things follow their natural course. Don't be overconfident. Seek help when it is required and

accept help when it is offered.

## Strength

Upright: Strength, Courage, Influence, Compassion, Persuasion

Reversed: Inner strength, Self-doubt, Low energy, raw emotion

The card shows the image of a woman stroking the forehead and jaws of a lion. The wild beast recognized for its ferociousness looks tame in her gentle and loving hands. The lion symbolizes raw passion and desire and the woman taming him is a representation that raw passion and desire can be channeled when tamed with strength and resilience which she uses to subtly tame the lion as opposed to force and domination. Her white robe signifies purity while her belt and crown of flowers represent the beauty of her expression of nature. The infinity symbol above her head signifies her infinite strength, wisdom, resilience, and potential.

Upright: The card in its base form represents strength, determination, and power similar to The Chariot. However, where The Chariot symbolizes outer strength, The Strength card signifies an inner strength and unbreakable spirit to persevere and overcome challenges. It signifies the mental strength required to overcome negative feelings like doubt, inadequacy, etc. The card also indicates a quiet but influential strength. One that doesn't control others but influences and guides them. The quiet strength is an advantage that lets you control things even when you don't seem in charge. The card encourages you to persevere even when all

hopes seems lost. The card also urges you to tame your instincts and gain more control over your emotions and channel them constructively. Don't let your emotions dictate your actions and reactions. Conquer your emotions and channel it to the benefit of everyone.

Reversed: The reversed strength card encourages you to find the strength within and apply it. Maybe you don't know it is there or you feel depleted that the strength you possess is infinite. It only stops if you let it, therefore don't give in to exhaustion but reconnect with your inner strength and resilience. Look to your past and remind yourself of how strong you are. Don't let doubt and fear run amok and take over. It can also represent the need to take a step back, relax and recharge yourself. You might be stretching yourself too thin and risk burning out.

In its worst interpretation, the reversed Strength can indicate a tendency to let your emotions control you causing you to harm yourself and others with your actions. It reminds you to be the master of your own emotions, actions, and reactions.

## The Hermit

Upright: Inner guidance, Introspection, Soul searching, Being alone,
Reversed: Loneliness, Isolation, Withdrawal

The Hermit stands atop a snow-capped mountain alone. The snowcapped range represents his growth, accomplishments and spiritual mastery. He has reached a pinnacle state of awareness due to the path of self-discovery he has chosen to take. A lantern containing a six-pointed star can be seen in his hands. The six-pointed star is a seal of Solomon, a symbol of wisdom. The lamplights the path The Hermit walks a few steps at a time. He doesn't see the whole journey except what is right in front of him but moves forward regardless to unravel the mysteries of the path. He holds a long staff in his other hand which he uses for guide and balance. The staff is a sign of his power and authority.

Upright: The Hermit indicates taking a breather from life and focusing your attention and energy inwards to find answers within. Knowledge and truth are found within and not in the distractions of life. You leave the known behind and venture out into the unknown in self- discovery with your inner wisdom your guiding light. You go on spiritual journeys so as to challenge your values, motivations, principles, and sense of self all in an effort to find your true self. You retreat into a private world either alone or with those of like minds and go on a journey to find your inner guiding light to illuminate the path to the answer you need and the wisdom you seek. Take a step at a time by seeing what is in your front rather than rushing to an end goal because there might be no end. The Hermit often appears at a point where you  are considering a new direction. You re-evaluate your personal goals and motivations by self-reflection, meditation, and contemplation to find a new path. You see the Universe from a place of deeper spiritual understanding and might, therefore, change some of your priorities. The Hermit can also appear as a spiritual guide or mentor to help you on your journey to higher self-awareness.

Reversed: it can represent the fact that you are either not engaging enough in internal reflection or you are overdoing it. The reversed Hermit can be telling you to take more time to reflect internally and connect with your spiritual self. Dig deeper and discover your greater purpose. Take time to meditate and do some soul searching. If you already spend time reflecting, then the reversed Hermit may be telling you that you are running the risk of closing yourself off to the world. Just as the connection to your inner self is important, your connections to others are just as important. Moderation is key, so don't become too self-

WHEEL of FORTUNE.

absorbed.

## Wheel of Fortune

Upright: Good luck, Life cycles, Destiny, Turning Point Reversed: Resistance to change, Bad luck, Breaking cycles

The Wheel of Fortune is a giant wheel as the name implies. Alchemic symbols are written on the inner wheels and they stand for Mercury, Sulphur, Water, and Salt which are the elementary units of life and the four elements that represent formative power. The outer wheel contains four Hebrew letters; "YHVN" (Yah Heh Vau Heh) which form the unutterable name of God. It also contains the letters "TORA" which can signify the word "Torah" meaning law. It can also be said to signify "ROTA" a Latin word for Wheel or it can even be "TAROT". Outside the wheel are; a Sphinx at the top which represents knowledge and strength. Anubis, the Egyptian god of the dead that welcomes souls of the dead to the underworld is on the right side. A snake is on the left side of the Wheel. The snake is Typhon, the Egyptian god of evil. The snake represents the life force plunging into the material world. Each corner of the card contains a winged creature each associated with four fixed zodiac signs; the angel is Aquarius, the eagle is Scorpio, the lion is Leo and the bull is

Taurus. Their wings shows stability amidst change and constant movement. Each of them holds a Torah which represents wisdom.

Upright: The Wheel of Fortune serves as a reminder that life is constantly changing just like a spinning wheel. So, if you are currently experiencing a hard time, be optimistic that there are better days ahead. Good luck and good fortune will come round. In contrast, it is a reminder that if you are currently enjoying a run of good luck, eventually things will return to normal. Therefore the card serves as a reminder to enjoy the great moments when they come around but remember that it can change and not lose hope when things are a bit difficult because things will always cycle back.

It is also a representation of the wheel of karma to remind you that "you reap what you sow" and "what goes around comes around". So endeavor to be kind and loving to people and the universe will reciprocate. And if you are not so good to people, that will also come back to you. It encourages you to be optimistic and never lose hope that things will turn out better. Be a beacon of good in your everyday interactions. Remember that sometimes, the way the universe cycles back will be out of your control and it might be difficult or even impossible to change it or interfere. So, just accept how it comes and go with the flow.

Reversed: A reversed Wheel of Fortune card signifies that things are taking a turn for the worst. You can let things play out, waiting for the wheel to cycle back in your favor or you can take action and be in charge of your destiny. That can start with acknowledging and owning your actions. This run of bad luck may be in response to the behaviors you have exhibited prior. Learn from these mistakes and apply the lessons so as not to make them again.

The reversed Wheel of Fortune also signifies a resistance to change. A change you don't want to accept has occurred and you want things to get back to how things are. This might not work out and you might need to accept the new situation and embrace it. On a positive note, the reversed Wheel of Fortune can be a sign that you are breaking a negative cycle that has been a part of you. You have finally let go of the negatives characteristics you exhibit and have finally broken free of the cycle.

Justice

Upright: Cause and Effect, Fairness, Truth, Law, Justice, Consequences Reversed: Unfairness, Dishonesty, Lack of Accountability

The Justice card has a woman sitting in front of a loosely hung purple veil which signifies compassion. She is between two pillars similar to those on the sides of the High Priestess and The Hierophant and the pillars symbolize balance, law, and structure.

In her right hand are a sword and a set of balance in her left hand. The sword signifies her logical and controlled mindset to dispense justice fairly. The sword is pointing upwards to signify a firm, final decision. The double-edge of the sword signifies that actions are always followed by consequences. The scale is on her intuitive hand (left hand). It shows that intuition must balance logic and represents impartiality. The woman wears a headpiece with a small square representing well-ordered thoughts and a red robe with a green mantle. The white shoe peeking beneath her clothes is a reminder of the spiritual consequences of actions.

Upright: The card represents justice, fairness truth and law. You are called to be judged as per your actions. If you have acted well and for the good of others and in synchronization with your Higher Self, you don't have anything to worry about. If not, then you will be called out on your actions. However, the Justice card is not Black and White. Compassion and Understanding temper Logic and Order. Therefore, the card suggests you will be treated fairly and without bias as you face the repercussions for your past actions. However, the raised sword about to strike down swiftly suggests that the consequences can be severe if necessary. Overall, the card is more about shouldering your actions and accepting the consequences. It can also mean that justice will be served if you are seeking it. You are to accept the decision of

Justice as there are no second chances with the upright Justice card.

The card also can appear when you are pondering over making an important decision with potential large scale repercussions. Choose wisely by reflecting on what your choice will mean for you and others. Connect with your intuition and seek a solution that works for the greatest good for yourself and others. Stand firmly by your decisions and accept the consequences that come with it. If you need to decide about something and you might not be willing to accept its consequences, dig deeper and seek another solution.

At its core, the card is about the search for truth. The more you discover the truth, the more you realize it is not just Black and White, so you will have to choose what truth is for you. Be prepared to accept that what is true might not be fair and ethical and vice versa. So be prepared to challenge the boundaries of your belief.

Reversed: The reversed Justice suggests that you may have done something that isn't morally right. You have a choice to either keep it secret or hope it remains so or own up to it, accept the consequences and take steps to resolve it. Whatever you choose, there will always be a consequence either from Justice or your conscience. The card also suggests that you may not want to accept responsibility and may try to shuffle it onto someone else. You are unwilling to look past your fears and ego and are being dishonest with yourself and others. The card calls you to assess the situation and accept your part of the blame in it and the responsibilities that come with that. Accept your mistakes and make it right so as to free yourself from guilt and shame. It also symbolizes that you are judging yourself too harshly. It reminds you to show yourself kindness and compassion and be willing to forgive yourself.

Also, if you have to come to a decision that will impact others,

the reversed Justice is a reminder not to make a judgment

based on bias or prejudice. Only make decisions that you are sure will truly serve justice. It also signals unfair or delayed justice coming to you.

## The Hanged Man

Upright: Letting go, Pause, New perspectives, Surrender Reversed: Stalling, Delays, Indecision, and Resistance

The Hanged Man shows a man hanging upside down from a T-shaped cross of living wood. The fact that he hangs upside down shows that he sees things from a perspective different from the norm. His expression is serene and calm which suggests that he is like that of his own choice.

The haloaround his head symbolizing awareness, enlightenment, and insight. His right foot is bound to the cross while his left foot is free and tucked bent behind his right leg. His hands are behind his back and his arms are folded to form an inverted triangle. His red pants represent human passion and physical body while his blue vest represents knowledge. The card is one of complete surrender, of being suspended in time, of martyrdom and sacrifice to the greater good.

Upright: it reminds you to stop what you are stuck on and move on before the Universe does it for you. Let the old ways be a thing of the past and try something new because change is inevitable and if you don't start it, it will happen and might be at an inconvenient time. It may be mental models or priorities or behavior, it is time to leave it and look at things from a new perspective and embrace the new opportunities that come with letting go of the old and accepting the new. The greater your synchronization with your intuition, the easier you can sense the signs of the pause and if you listen to it, then the Universe would not have to do it for you often in clear but not so fun ways.

The Hanged Man's appearance can symbolize a project or activity may be ending. Surrender to the opportunity to pause and re-assess and find a new perspective rather than forcibly pushing forward. Something new might be emerging that you might not see if you are too focused on the old and this is your chance to discover it. Take time from your routine and connect to a different way of seeing the world. You may be temporarily putting important things on hold but it will eventually be worth it. It can also be a reflection that you a currently stuck in your current situation. It asks you to let go and flow with the current of life. Or you can shift your energy to something other than your routine and gain a new perspective on the world around you.

Reversed: The reversed Hanged Man shows you that you are resisting the known need to hit the pause button. You keep yourself busy with routine so as not to face issues that need your attention. Your spirit and body ask you to stop but you are ignoring it and your mind keeps racing. Remember, the world has a way of having its way and forcing a pause, so do it yourself before it is too late. You may be frustrated because you are currently in a position where everything is on hold. The card is suggesting that it is advisable to surrender what is and let go of your hold to how things are. It can also represent the time to advance with a new perspective and energy if you've been on hold. You may have finally found a breakthrough or new realization. It can also mean you are stalling and important decisions as you don't feel fully ready but the card is a sign to take the brave choice to move on and make the decision.

## Death

Upright: Endings, Change, Transition, Transformation

Reversed: Inner Purging, Personal Transformation, and Resistance
 to change.

The card depicts the Messenger of Death. A skeleton in black armor atop a white horse carrying a black flag decorated with a white five-petal rose. The skeleton represents the part of the body that survives afterlife has left it. The armor symbolizes invincibility and the fact that death comes regardless, its dark coloring is that of mourning and mysteriousness while the horse is the color of purity and is a sign of strength and power. The five-petal rose on the flag reflects beauty, immortality, and purification and the number "five" represents change. All of these symbols tell us that death is not just about the end of life. It is about birth and rebirth, endings and beginnings, change and transformation. Death is part of life and there is a beauty to be found in it.

A dead royal figure can be seen on the ground while a bishop, a young woman, and a child seemingly plead with Death presumably to spare them but at the end of it all, Death gets everybody. In the background is a boat sailing down a river similar to mythological tales of boats escorting the dead to the afterlife. The Sun is set between two towers over the horizon in a sense of being born every morning and dying every night. This mirrors a depiction of the Moon Tarot card.

Upright: The Death card is the most feared in the deck and the most misunderstood. Most people take the card literally ad believe that card represents an actual death. In reality, the card can be a positive card.

After the pause and reflection of the Hanged Man, the Death card symbolizes the end of a major era in your life that is no longer necessary for your growth and therefore opens up the possibility of something new that is more valuable and essential. The past must be put down and left behind for a new future of hope and possibilities to be embraced. More than anything, the Death card signifies the inevitability of endings and change. It may be difficult to let go but the importance of doing so will be revealed with the promise of transformation and renewal. If you resist the inevitable endings, you may experience pain, both physically and emotionally.

Therefore Death shows a time of major transition, transformation, and change. The change should be seen as a positive, cleansing transformation. The death and clearing away of the past can open the door to a brighter and more satisfying life journey. The Death card can imply sudden, unexpected changes just as literal death can be. So, the Death card can be a sign of being caught in a sudden change that can't be controlled or altered (especially if drawn along with the Tower and the Hanged Man cards). This change might be painful initially but it also brings about new opportunities and perspectives.

Reversed: The reversed Death can be a sign of resistance to change. A sign of not letting go or not knowing how to. You want to carry the baggage of your past into the future and are therefore stuck. This card gives you the chance to embrace change and not resist it. Take a chance on the possibilities that come with change. As you let the past go and give yourself to the present, the future gets brighter. On a deeper level, the reversed Death card can be a sign of you undergoing a massive personal transition often in private. You are releasing what is no longer necessary and thereby creating space for something new. The change can be physical or mental but it is a necessary one that you will come out the better from.

## Temperance

Upright: Patience,Moderation, Purpose, Balance Reversed: Self-healing, Excess, Re-alignment, Imbalance
This card depicts a large winged angel who appears to be not just masculine but also feminine. She dons a light blue robe with a triangle enclosed in a square on the front. This represents that humans (triangle) are bound by Earth and its natural laws

(square). The angel is balanced with one leg on the stones and the other in the water. The foot on the stones symbolizes the need to stay grounded and the one in the water symbolizes the need to flow. She is pouring water between two cups symbolizing the flow and alchemy of life.

In the background, a winding path up a mountain can be seen, representing life's journey. A gold crown encased in golden light hovers above the mountain symbolizing the taking of a higher path and staying true to one's life purpose and meaning.

Upright: The Temperance card brings with it balance, patience and moderation. You are being reminded to stabilize your energy and let life flow through you without resistance. Recover your flow and get order and balance back in your life. Remain calm even through the stress of life. Control your emotions and temperament. Respect balance and tranquility and let your patience help you control your temperament with regards to the little things.

Take the middle path and accommodate all views. Don't be opinionated or controversial. Be a peacekeeper and keep the balance. Avoid extremes. Create harmony among a diverse group of people and work together to leverage the mix of strengths and weaknesses to be found.

The card is about the alchemy of diverse elements to create something new and better than its individual parts. Take your time to do your best. Take a moderate and guided approach to your goals. The card also reflects higher learning. You are learning, your conscience is helping you get the optimal outcome and you are listening and following with patience.

Reversed: The reversed Temperance card is a warning or invitation for you to restore balance and moderation of you have been indulging in excesses. It may be drinking, eating, fighting, buying, partying, etc. These excesses take you away from your true self and what you can achieve, your greatest potential. So, stop the excesses or maybe even abstain from it completely so as to restore balance back in your life. The reverse Temperance can represent that things aren't right with your life and therefore creating tension and stress. There is a voice deep within telling you things aren't right and you will do well to listen, re-align and re-adjust yourself to find your flow once more. It also reflects a period of self-evaluation and a time to reassess your priorities so you can shed the excesses weighing you down. You might still be involved in things that will not add anything to you in terms of your future goals and aspirations. Some of them might even be positive things but they have no place in the future you envision for yourself, so they are excess and you need to leave it. The balance and moderation you attain from heeding the warnings of the reversed Temperance card will open you to the possibility of self-healing and create more flow in your life.

Devil

Upright: Attachment, Sexuality, Addiction, Shadow self, Restriction, Reversed: Detachments, Exploring dark thoughts, Releasing limiting beliefs

The card shows Baphomet, a half goat, half man being. Baphomet was initially a sign of balance between human and animal, good and bad, male and female. Recently though, it has been used to represent the occult and has become a scapegoat for things considered evil.

The Devil has the wings of a vampire bat, a creature known for sucking the lifeblood of its prey and this represents a symbolism of what occurs when you give in to raw desires. His entrancing stare hypnotizes those who come close and place them under his influence. The inverted pentagram is above him, a symbol of occultism and dark magic. His right hand is raised in the Vulcan salute, a Jewish blessing and in his left is a torch that is on fire.

At the Devil's feet is a man and woman, chained at the neck naked to the podium the Devil sits on. While they might appear chained against their will, the looseness of the chain suggests that they can break free if they choose to. They each have a small horn on their heads similar to the Devil, showing that they are gradually becoming like him. They have tails that further symbolize their raw instincts and animalistic nature, while the grapes and fire on their tails symbolize pleasure and lust.

Upright: The Devil card represents your darker nature (shadow side) and the negative elements restricting you from being the best part of yourself. You may be at the hooks of negative habits and find yourself trapped between its short, fleeting pleasure and its long term pain. Just as the Lovers card symbolizes choice and duality, so does the Devil card. However, with this cards, you are picking fleeting pleasure despite the lengthy repercussions and in effect, selling your soul to the Devil.

The devil card appears when you feel you have no control over your dark side and can't help but indulge. However, deep down you know it is you who continues to make these choices that cause detriment to you and those close to you. To break free, you have to tell this truth to yourself and acknowledge it. The Devil card presents you with an opportunity to bring the negative influences around you to the forefront so you can take action and free yourself its shackles. Shine the light on them so their grip on you may loosen and you make the conscious effort to remove yourself from the grip.

On a brighter note, the Devil card can be a sign of a powerful attachment between two individuals. A romance in its honeymoon period. It can be one between lovers, new friends, a mother and a newborn, etc. However, remember the lesson of the Temperance card of moderation because, with the appearance of the Devil card, even a healthy attachment can rapidly descend into an unhealthy one if you lose a sense of yourself. It also symbolizes the wilder side of your sexuality and your need to explore it. Set boundaries and don't let it entrap you and sink you into its darker side.

Reversed: A reverse Devil card is a call to free yourself of negative limiting beliefs that hold you back from your highest potential. It reminds that you must deal with your darker side before you can grow. Confront your inner fears and escape from the chains of self-doubt and limitations that hold you back. Take the opportunity to bring about a positive turnaround in your life. The reverse Devil card also signifies that it's time for you to confront your deepest and darkest. You are doing so consciously and from a place of strength, courage and utmost confidence. You seek understanding of your innermost self either so you can conquer it or so you can integrate and channel it positively. This may be the new better version of yourself you were searching for.

The card also encourages you to practice detachment in the sense of the Buddhist principle in which you rise above your attachment to the desires of things, people and concepts of the world and remove yourself from its restrictions. You still care for people but are free of your dependence on the, their opinions, their approval, etc.

The Tower

Upright: Upheaval, Revelation, Sudden change, Chaos, Awakening

Reversed: Averting disaster, Fear of change, Personal

transformation

The Tower card depicts a tall tower atop a rocky mountaintop. Lightning has struck the Tower alight and two people (a man and woman) leap out of the building with arms outstretched in a scene depicting destruction and chaos. The Tower is a sturdy structure that has been constructed on rocky foundations causing a single bolt of lightning strike to bring it crashing down. It represents goals and ambitions made on a false premise. The lightning represents the surge of insight that causes a revelation or breakthrough. It enters from the highest point of the tower and knocks its crown off symbolizing energy flowing down the universe via the crown chakra nodes. The people are panicked in their bid to escape even though they don't know what awaits them at the bottom of the fall. The 12 Zodiac signs and 10 Tree of Life points are symbolized by the 22 flames and they suggest divine intervention even in periods of disaster.

Upright: The Tower card asks you to brace for the unexpected; chaos, upheaval, massive change. It can come in any form; death, divorce, job loss, natural disaster. The effect will shake you at your core and affect you physically, mentally and spiritually. It can't be dodged. It can't be escaped. It can't be avoided. Change is here like a whirlwind to upend you.

However, it is ultimately for your Highest Good.

As you settle into safety and comfort, the Tower huts and throws you for a loop as a lightning bolt of insight breaks through the illusions you have been convincing yourself are real and the real truth comes to light. Your world may come crashing down as you come to the realization that it was built on shaky foundations; lies, illusions, false assumptions, etc. All you believed to be true has turned on its head and you now question what to believe. This is even more disorienting if core beliefs are the ones shaken. However, over time you will come to see that your original beliefs were based on false understandings and appreciate the opportunity to cultivate new beliefs more grounded in reality. Give in and let the structure collapse so you can rebuild. Surrender is the best option with the Tower card as it brings with it inevitable upheavals you have no chance against. You will have to trust that it is all happening for a reason. The destruction will allow new growth to emerge and you will come out stronger, wiser and more resilient as your perspective changes. This moment is necessary for the advancement of your spiritual journey even though it involves pain.

In its best form, if you are in synchronization with your Higher Self, The Tower can simply be a sign of spiritual awakening as you preemptively see the cracks in your beliefs which allows you take proactive action before it all comes crashing down. The inevitable change still occurs but you can direct it so it causes minimal damage.

Reversed: The reversed Tower implies that you're going through a major personal transformation. Unlike the upright card where the change is caused by external forces and mostly out of your control, with the reverse card, you are causing the change and challenging your beliefs, values, and purpose. Your spiritual journey takes you on a new path and it may cause you to change your opinions about important topics. It might be a case of an existential crisis where you seriously question who you are and your purpose in life. It is all good if you trust the process and allow the change and transformation to evolve you into a better version of yourself.

At times, the reversed Tower card can be a sign of resisting the inevitable change. You remain in denial and hold on tightly to your crumbling beliefs. Know that the change will eventually find its way to upend your life no matter how long you hold it at bay. Just like the upright card, the reverse card can a warning to those who can see it as such, those in sync with their Higher Self. It is a warning of change to come and they prepare for it.

Star

Upright: Faith, Hope, Purpose, Spirituality, Renewal Reversed: Disconnection, Despair, Lack of faith, Self-trust

The Star card depicts a fully naked woman kneeling by the edge of a small body of water. In each hand is a container filled with water; the left (subconscious) and the right (conscious).

She pours water from one container to sustain the earth and continue its fertility cycle represented by the vibrant greenery around. The other container pours water on dry land in fie rivulets symbolizes the senses. She has one foot on land and the other in the water. The foot on land represents practical abilities and common sense while the other one represents intuition, listening to inner voices and channeling inner resources. Her nakedness represents her vulnerability and purity while under a vast starry night sky. One large star shines behind her presenting her core essences and the seven smaller stars represent the chakras.

Upright: The Star following the Tower is a welcome change from the destruction and turmoil. The challenge brought about by change has been endured, you have shed illusions and are now finding your true self. The Star brings rejuvenated hope, faith and a sense of blessing by the Universe. You now enter a new place in your life brimming with peace, mental stability, love, calm energy and a greater understanding of yourself and others. This is the turning point of your personal growth and development. Anything is possible and you are full of hope and your soul is uplifted to the highest as you realize the possibility of your dreams being achievable. It is time to allow yourself dream and aspire towards the stars.

It is time to get your sense of purpose and meaning to life again. You are changing and transforming yourself into the best version you can be. Open yourself to new ideas and perspectives. The Star suggests a generous demeanor. You want to share yourself with others and help them transform as you have done. You feel like giving back to the Universe the blessings you have received from it.

Reversed: The reversed Star card indicates that you have lost faith and hope in the Universe. You feel over-encumbered by life's problems and feel shortchanged by all that is happening to you as you feel too much too fast. Your calls to the Universe to ease up on you seem unanswered and you wonder if the Divine is looking out for you. You should pay attention and see the deeper lessons and see how your present situation is a blessing. The reverse Star card can signify a test of faith to see if you crumble or stand firmly when faced with challenges. You should trust yourself and the challenges. You should trust yourself and the Universe and let your strong faith and confidence allow the Divine to shine through you.

The reverse Star card also be represent a lack of inspiration and disengagement from life. You great vision and aspiration that excited you once is now being overwhelmed by boring routine, so it might be time to make a change. You can move on or you can reconnect with that which is truly important to you. Sync your life with your purpose and dream and you can find inspiration.

The Moon

Upright: Illusion, Anxiety, Fear Intuition, Subconscious Reverse: Release of fear, Inner Confusion, Repressed Emotion

It shows a night sky with a full moon positioned between two towers. The moonlight doesn't shine as bright as that of the sun. The moon symbolizes intuition, the unconscious and dreams. Its dimmer light just slightly illuminates the road to higher consciousness twisting between the towers.

In the foreground, there is a small pool representing the watery subconscious and the small crayfish crawling out of it symbolizes the initial stages of unfolding consciousness. The tamed and wild aspects of the mind are symbolized by the dog and wolf on the grassy field howling at the moon.

Upright: The moon represents fears and illusions especially when you are using your past experiences to project fears on your present and into your future. This mostly stems from past hurts that were pushed down to the subconscious and are now re-surfacing and are affecting you consciously or unconsciously. It is time to synchronize with your subconscious and deal with the fears and anxiety rooted in your past experience. The Moon card can also represent uncertainty and illusion when things might not be as they seem. Be wary of making quick decisions as they might end up being based on half-truths, misinformation, etc. Trust your intuition to help you see what is beyond the obvious. Let go of the conscious mental barriers and allow your intuition to be free to guide you. If you listen, your intuition can guide you to higher levels of enlightenment and understanding. Your intuition will help you interpret the message of the subconscious.

Also, when the Moon card appears, pay close heed to the lunar cycles and synchronize with its Divine powers. Connect with the Divine and discover intuitive insights of what lies beyond the ordinary. Set your intuitions and plant seeds of opportunities on the New Moon while on the Full Moon, honor your achievements and look at things needed let go of so you can grow.

Reversed: The reversed Moon indicates that you are dealing with fears, illusions, and anxiety. You are sorting through them, understanding how they affect you and working to free yourself from their negative impact. Due to this, their effect on you is subsiding and you are undergoing a liberating and transformative experience.

The reversed Moon also shows that you might be receiving intuitive messages but struggle to interpret the meanings. The message itself may be confusing or your interpretation may differ across different scenarios causing confusion. It is high time to listen to your conscience and trust that the answers you need are already within you. Record your dreams and the messages you got so you can come back to them from a position of clarity and better understanding.

The Sun

Upright: Warmth, Vitality, Positivity, Fun, Success Reversed: Inner child, Overly optimistic, Feeling down

The Sun card radiates positivity and optimism. A big sun shines brightly in the sky and it represents the origin of all life. Four sunflowers grow on a brick wall symbolizing the four suits of the Minor Arcana and the four elements. A young naked child atop a gentle white horse is in the foreground. The child symbolizes the joy of being in sync with the inner spirit and his nakedness represents the purity and innocence of childhood and is a sign of having nothing to hide. The white horse is a sign of purity and strength.

Upright: The Sun card represents radiance, success, and abundance. It strengthens you and encourages you to be positive and radiant regardless of what you do as this will bring joy into your life. Others will be naturally drawn to your bright, positive, optimistic energy and that energy will get you through the tough times. Your energy can be shared with others, so shine your love and positivity with others around you. The Sun card signifies that things will get better if you are having a hard time as the sun is the ultimate light at the end of the tunnel.

Every challenge on your path has made you grow and evolve and you will soon reap the fruit of your perseverance.

The Sun synchronizes you to your base power, the abundant inner energy that radiates through you and you can tap into it using your Divine will to express it in positive ways. The Sun card represents a time when your physical vitality and positivity will increase as the card is an energetic one.

Reversed: The reversed Sun calls on your inner child. As adults, we tend to forget how to have fun in all the rigors and challenges of life. The reversed Sun is encouraging you to leave your routine if just for a while and have the carefree kind of fun that a kid would. Let your heart and soul fly free and free yourself of the worries and concerns of life.

The reversed Sun can also indicate that your optimism and enthusiasm are low. You are going through challenges that are making it unable for you to see the brighter side of life. Your path seems clouded and you are unable to see past that to believe that things will eventually work out. However, remember that the sun never stops shining, so this is all temporary. Have a little faith and you will eventually see that the hurdles in your path are scalable and your dreams achievable.

At its worst, the reversed Sun card is a sign of overconfidence or over-optimism. You are being egoistical and your confidence is no longer coming from hard work and faith but from arrogance and pride. Remember to be grounded in reality even in your most confident times.

Judgment

Upright: Absolution, Rebirth, Inner calling, Judgment Reversed: Ignoring the call, Inner critic, Self-doubt

The card depicts naked people, including children, all rising up from their different graves, looking skywards with their arms outstretched. Above is the archangel Gabriel and he is blowing a trumpet. The people below are responding to the call and waiting to see if they will be accepted into heaven after being judged. The background has an extensive range of mountains signifying insurmountable challenges and unavoidable call for judgment.

Upright: The judgment card can often signal the need to make a life-altering decision that would require a combination of intuition and intellect. You may be at the crossroads ready to make this life-changing decision that carries long term effects and consequences. Trust your judgment and believe that you are walking the right path. Tune in to your Higher Self and let your past life lessons guide you. You have reached a major stage in your journey. You have learned from the past and have gained absolution from its lessons. You have released yourself from regrets and guilt and are ready to step into the future with its new challenges.

The card also suggests that you will find comfort in sharing your struggles in a controlled group with those who have had a similar experience. Let them guide and help you.

Reversed: Reflection and Self-evaluation. With meditation and contemplation, you gain deep understandings of the weavings of the universe around you. You may fear the judgment of people which has prompted you to keep secrets hidden. Work on self-acceptance and self- forgiveness.

The reversed Judgment card can also appear when you are ignoring messages from the universe. You might be afraid of not being worthy enough to answer the call or worried about the sacrifice it will entail. The call never goes away, therefore push past your self-doubts and insecurities and trust that the universe called you for a reason. The card can also mean your inner critic shouting out loud and clear. This is the underlying reason for your self-doubt and insecurities and it is limiting you from fulfilling your potential. Separate your inner critic from yourself. Acknowledge its valid criticism and focus on breaking from the cycle of self- criticism by replacing it with positive reinforcements.

The World

Upright: Completion, Accomplishments, Travel, Integration

Reversed: Seeking personal closure, Shortcuts, Delays

The World card depicts a naked woman partially wrapped in purple cloth dancing inside a laurel wreath. She is looking back to her past as her body dances forward into the future. Her hands hold two wands like that of magicians. This symbolizes the Magician's manifestations

finally coming to fruition with the world. The circular shape of the wreath symbolizes the continuous cycle of successful completions and new beginnings as the woman is ending a phase and beginning another almost simultaneously.

The wreath is surrounded by four symbols which are similar to the Wheel of Fortune as both cards allude to the cycle of life and progression through it. The four figures are; a Lion, a Bull, a Cherub and an Eagle. They symbolize the four fixed signs of the zodiac; Leo, Taurus, Aquarius, and Scorpio. They are also represent the four suits of the Tarot, the four points of the compass, the four seasons, the four elements and the four corners of the universe. All this guides you from one phase to another and brings balance to your journey.

Upright: When the World card appears, you have attained fulfillment, completion, and achievements. It might be graduation, marriage, achieving a long-held dream, etc. It has all come together and everything is right with the world. You feel whole and complete and you have a sense of closure and accomplishments. Therefore, the card invites you to reflect on your journey until now. Celebrate your accomplishments and bask in the joy it brings. All the trails and obstacles have made you stronger, wiser and more experienced. Take time to celebrate the conclusion of the journey before you begin a new one. Look back and acknowledge how far you have come, and consolidate what you have learned. This reflection will serve as a building block when you finally start a new phase. If loose ends remain, the World card implores you to complete them. Take the final step needed to reach the finish line so you have the time and space for new beginnings and opportunities.

More literally, the card can signify travel. You might have a chance to travel from your comfort zone and see new parts of the world. This can serve as a reinforcement of your understanding of the universe and provide you a greater appreciation of its beauty.

Reversed: The reversed World suggests that you might be seeking closure. You want to move on from an emotionally charged dream, aspiration or situation. You have accepted the inevitability of the change that has occurred and are ready to embrace the new reality. The reverse World can also signify your need to complete a phase but an unwillingness to take the necessary steps. You want to skip through the trials and challenges which are necessary for you to gain a sense of achievement and completion. Don't be afraid to test your limits even through hardships and challenges as they make victory even sweeter.

The card also reminds you not to lose focus especially at the final lap of the phase you are experiencing e.g. a project. Re-energize and find new focus by reminding yourself of the sweetness of victory. The reverse world can also mean a delay in completion. Get creative and find new ways to scale the hurdle preventing you from reaching your goals.

The Cards of the Minor Arcana

As earlier stated, there are 56 cards in the minor arcana over four suits. Going by the Rider- Waite-Smith deck, the cards are arranged thus:

Suits of Swords

*Ace of Swords*

Upright: New ideas, Breakthroughs, Success, Mental clarity

Reversed: Inner clarity, Clouded judgment, Re-thinking an idea

The Ace of Swords depicts a gleaming hand appearing from a cloud which represents the Divine. The hand holds a sword upright and this symbolizes mind and intellect. At the tip of the sword sits a wreath draped crown which is a sign of victory and success. Though the Ace is a sign of triumph, the jagged mountain in the background suggests a challenging road ahead that will need mental resilience to be navigated.

Upright: This card signifies new energy from the intellectual realm. You may be on the edge of a major breakthrough or way of thinking that forces you to see everything from a new perspective. Reinforce your mental energy through meditation and use your intellectual potential to the fullest. The Ace of Swords signifies that you are mentally ready to start something new especially things that require mental power and intellect.

The Ace of Swords also represents power as sword cards do and the double-edge of the sword implies the duality of its ability to create and destroy. Therefore, it represents power and responsibilities. So, you can wield your power for the greatest good rather than not. The card encourages you to pursue truth and justice. Stand up for your causes and people.

Reversed: The reversed Ace of Swords indicates new ideas you aren't willing to share yet. You are yet to fully express the idea within yourself, so you are not ready to manifest it to the world. So, give yourself time to understand this budding idea before sharing it. Sometimes it is a signal that you have an idea not coming to fruition as you have been expecting.

It might an idea you are no longer interested in. Or it might be that you can't settle on an idea, so it is time to step back and reassess. Do some planning and have a clear image of the goal you want to achieve. The card also suggests a lack of mental clarity or clouded judgment.

Take a breather to get your head together and gather all the information before you proceed.

*Two of Swords*

Upright: Weighing options, Difficult decisions, Impasse, Avoidance

Reversed: Stalemate, Indecision, Information overload, Confusion

The Two of Swords depicts a sitting, blindfolded woman adorned in a white robe and holding two swords crossed. The blindfold indicates confusion about her plight as she sees neither problem nor solution clearly. The swords indicate weighing of thoughts and taking into account both sides of a dilemma as they are held in perfect balance.

A stretch of water with jagged islands are behind her. The water represents emotion and this is symbolic to the woman using her heart in conjunction with her head in making decisions as the sword card is known for mind and intellect. The island represents the obstacles to be scaled and the crescent moon to her right signifies that she needs to trust her intuition.

Upright: The card indicates that you are wrestling with a decision on a challenging situation. The options seem part good and part bad and you are confused about which will lead to an optimal outcome. Weigh both options using your head and heart and choose the path that aligns most with your Higher Self.

Just as the woman in the cards is blindfolded indicating a lack of awareness of her surroundings, you might also be missing something. Like a crucial piece of information or an alternative solution. Find your way out of your lack of awareness and remove the blindfold. Seek guidance, research more and look further inwards to find this missing piece. The blindfold can also indicate that you are purposefully blinding yourself from making a choice or you are hoping to make a random choice. Remember that you can't ignore a problem and hope it goes away and your choices have consequences, so it is better to decide on a logical and informed choice and not a random one. Avoid indecision or impasse.

Reversed: The reversed card suggests you have a tough decision to make. You feel all the options presented will likely lead to negative outcomes and therefore find it difficult to make a choice. You are stuck and unable to proceed. You may lack the information to make an adequate choice or there is so much information that it is difficult for you to know which one to act upon. Listen to your intuition, your intuition and tune out the worldly noise. Trust your wisdom and let your internal compass guide you.

The card also represents a stalemate. You are butting heads and are unable to reach a compromise. Remove the blinders, take a step back and look at issues from the perspective of the other side. You could also be stuck between two competing sides and you are confused about how to maintain the peace. Find a way to broker peace or leave the situation especially if your presence is not a necessary factor.

*Three of Swords*

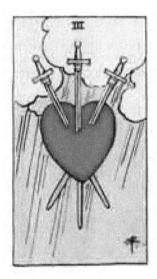

Upright: Heartbreak, Emotional pain, Sorrow, Hurt, Grief

Reversed: Negative self-talk, Releasing pain, Optimism,

Forgiveness

The Three of Swords depict a heart stabbed by three swords and this represents the emotional and physical pain inflicted by intent, words, and actions. The dark cloud in the background mirrors the pain but also brings hope that pain and hurt will eventually disappear just like dark clouds do.

Upright: The Three of Swords signals a deep hurt and disappointment. Your heart has figuratively been stabbed by people's words, intentions and actions and as it so often happens, it was sudden and unexpected. The card is about going through the emotions. Express your sadness and disappointment. Don't hold it in. Letting it go is a part of the process. Grief, accept and move on. Pain and sorrow are part of the life cycle and the experience is a life lesson that will make you stronger. The pain will eventually pass and you will come from the experience stronger.

Reversed: The reversed Three of Swords asks you to reflect on your self-talk and self- criticism. Your words to yourself have the power to shape you, so reinforce yourself with positive words of encouragement. Don't let negative thoughts be your driving force. Likewise for the negativity and criticism of others towards you. While it is good to take note of the criticism of others and make amends where necessary, don't let those who criticize for the sake of it bring you down.

The card can also signal a silver lining. The light at the end of the tunnel. You have gone through a bad patch and are coming out the other side.

*Four of Swords*

Upright: Meditation, Recuperation, Contemplation, Rest and relaxation Reversed: Burn out, Exhaustion, Stagnation, Deep contemplation

The Four of Swords depicts a knight lying down in a tomb in full armor with his hands folded in like in prayer as a sign of rest. One sword lies beneath him while three hang above him pointing downwards towards his head and torso. The sword beneath him symbolizes a single point of focus. The stained windows above show a woman and child together.

Upright: The Four of Swords card reminds you to take a rest between phases. Rest and re- energize so you are able to give a hundred percent in the next phase. Constant stress without rest will break you, so make rest a priority. Take a break from work, making decisions and so on. Re-vitalize your mental strength through meditation and enjoy peace and tranquility.

The card is also a suggestion to review where you are, where you have been and where you are going. As you are resting, re-assess or re-affirm your priorities. Evaluate what has been done, what can be done better and what needs to change.

Reversed: Where the upright card is reminding you to rest, the reverse card is telling you to rest. You are close to burning out and the demand on you is at the breaking point that you can endure. It is time to take a step back from everything and retreat from the world.

The card also suggests stagnation. You are currently at a point where things aren't moving forward and it is frustrating. This can be due to your passive approach and you are feeling the consequences of that choice.

*Five of Swords*

Upright: Disagreement, Winning at all costs, Conflict, Defeat, Competition Reversed: Making amends, Reconciliation, Past resentments

The card depicts a man picking three swords from the ground. He is looking back over his shoulder to two other men walking away from two swords on the ground with slumped shoulders suggesting a fought and lost battle. The cloudy and tumultuous sky signifies that all is not well even though the fighting has ended.

Upright: The card is a sign that you are walking from a situation with a sense of sadness and loss. It doesn't matter if you won or lost out in that situation, argument or disagreement, you have seen that the cost of the battle is higher than whatever you might have gained from fighting it. The card, therefore, advises you to choose your battles and not get into every conflict that comes your way. Be sure to prioritize the important things over the need to have an argument. If you already got into a conflict you regret, be willing to admit your regrets and your fault. Find a compromise in your disagreement and seek to put things behind you.

The card can also be a sign of impending failure or you doing anything to win even if it means stepping on others. Don't let the losses keep you down and remember that what goes around comes around eventually.

Reversed: The reversed card can indicate conflict following you after you have attempted to move on and this is interfering with your need to move forward. The card is also an indication that it is time to make amends and reconcile with those who your relationship with has deteriorated due to unnecessary conflict.

You may still have resentment over a past disagreement and the unresolved feelings are causing a facture in your relationship with the person on the other side. It also indicates the end of a conflict and time to move forward after repairing the past.

*Six of Swords*

Upright: Transition, Change, Releasing baggage, Rite of passage
Reversed: Unfinished business, Resistance to change, Personal transition

The Six of Swords card depicts a woman and child as they are rowed across the water to land. The woman's head is covered and downcast suggesting loss or sadness. The child stays close to her for comfort. In the boat stands six swords signifying past baggage being carried on the journey to the future. The water nearby is turbulent while the one ahead is calm signifying leaving behind a dangerous situation for a more peaceful one.

Upright: The card is a sign that you are in a period of transition, leaving the past behind and moving into the future. The change might be of your choice or forced by circumstances. You might feel sad about the change but you know it is necessary especially if the past you are leaving behind is a turbulent one and you are going forward into a promised better future. So, the cards ask you to free yourself of past baggage you might be carrying into this future. Let the past remain there and head into the future free of it.

Reversed: The reversed Six of Swords suggest you are experiencing a personal transition aimed at changing things that have no place in your future. You are taking a personal journey aimed at changing yourself. It can also indicate the need to change but also the reluctance to do so. You are holding on to the past or hoping things can get better without you changing.

Push past your comfort zone and move forward. Don't be scared to make a change.

The card also suggests unresolved conflict from your past holding you back and holding you back from moving on. Maybe lessons you haven't learned or conflicts yet to be resolved.

*Seven of Swords*

Upright: Betrayal, Getting away with something, Deception, Strategic action Reversed: Self-deceit, Imposter syndrome, Keeping secrets

The card depicts a man as he is slinking away from a military building. He has five swords in his arms while another two swords are stuck in the ground that he looks at over his shoulder. He looks pleased with himself.

Upright: The Seven of Swords traditionally indicate deception, theft, trickery, and betrayal. You may be keeping a secret, sneaking around or trying to get away with something. You might get away with it or you might get caught. There will likely be a huge fallout if you do get caught and the effort required to possibly get away with it is immense. So, it might not be worth it in the end. In another interpretation, the card can be a sign that you might be a victim of imminent betrayal, especially from a trusted individual. Be at alert and listen to your intuition.

The card could also be suggesting that you will be served better if you approach things strategically. Prioritize, delegate and find creative ways to solve your problems. However, be aware of using backdoors and not following due process. That may be a bad idea that could have severe consequences.

Reversed: The reversed Seven of Swords appears at a time you suffer imposter syndrome where you believe you are not good enough. This is when you need to trust yourself and stop manifesting your doubts. The card alsos suggest that you are attempting to convince yourself of something you don't believe in. It can also suggest hidden, dark secrets that are causing you worries of guilt and shame. Free yourself of this burden. Start by forgiving yourself and opening up to those you trust.

*Eight of Swords*

Upright: Negative thoughts, Imprisonment, Victim mentality

Reversed: Releasing negative thoughts, Inner critic, Open to a new perspective

The card depicts a woman trapped and surrounded by eight swords. She is blindfolded and bound. This symbolizes limiting thoughts and mindset that prevents her from moving forward. The free space in her front suggests that a way out for her exists even if she can't see it yet. The water at her feet suggests that her intuition might be able to guide her where sight cannot.

Upright: The card suggests that you feel trapped by circumstances and cannot see a way out. You are between the devil and the deep blue sea. However, just like the free space in the blindfolded woman's front, there is a way out for you even if you don't see it yet. You have to take off the "blindfold" that is restricting you. The card can also refer a warning that you are overthinking and limiting yourself by only considering what can go wrong. Get out of your head, find some perspective, replace negative thoughts with positive ones and start creating favorable situations for yourself. There is a way out. It's up to you to find it. The card can be associated with victim mentality in which you allow yourself to stay trapped by external forces waiting to be rescued rather than helping yourself.

Reversed: You hold beliefs that prevent you from finding a goal much less achieve it. You give up before you even start due to your negative self-talk and self-criticism. The reversed card asks you to break this cycle of negative pattern thought.

On a positive note, the reversed card can be a sign of you letting go of negative and self- limiting beliefs and attitudes. You are now open to self-acceptance and change.

CPSIA information can be obtained
at www.ICGtesting.com
Printed in the USA
LVHW080924260421
685569LV00011B/833